FEEDBACK THAT WORKS

FEEDBACK THAT WORKS

to your children, colleagues, staff, boss, spouse....

PHILIPPE GRAFF

ISBN: 1503273350
ISBN 13: 9781503273351

FEEDBACK THAT WORKS

CHAPTER 1

What is Feedback ?

Feedback is a reaction to an opinion, a fact or an experience given by the person who has been exposed to that opinion, fact or experience.

It can be given orally, in writing, through verbal or non verbal signals or through an action (sending of a gift for example).

Feedback can be solicited or unsolicited.

Here are four different examples of feedback :

- I spend a night in a hotel and my feedback is solicited by the hotel management: I fill the requested questionnaire and gives it to the reception

- One of my colleagues does something I do not appreciate and I decide to react: I send him an email to express my discontent.

- The concert was excellent and the public applauds: the musicians play one or more "encore".

- My life companion acts as if he was alone so I prepare myself to share my negative feelings with him: I provoke a discusssion to share my feelings.

These different situations describe a feedback process. In some cases it is positive, in others it is negative.

Generally speaking it is easier to give positive feedback because it is appreciated by most people and therefore safer than negative feedback that may provoke negative reactions.

Although it is generally well accepted, positive feedback may sometimes be rejected by some people who suspect negative intentions or feel that the positive feedback that they received was not genuine.

This is why we should think carefully before giving either positive or negative feedback and ask ourselves a few questions like:

Is the feedback I intend to give deserved ? Will it be appreciated ?

Is it the right time to give it or should I wait for a better occasion ?

Is the person I want to give it to capable of taking it ?

Does she need it, want it ?

One should be particularly cautious when giving positive feedback to very sensitive people and make sure that it is genuine and deserved.

Faced with a negative reaction to positive feedback, the best is to explain the reason why we felt like expressing this positive feedback, hoping that our explanation will dissipate any misunderstanding.

Negative feedback is more complex to give than positive feedback because it is often not well received for many reasons that we will consider.

However negative feedback, provided it is given in a constructive way, should be considered as a gift rather than a vexation.

Because, when given well, it allows the recipient to become aware of how his opinion, action, decision has been perceived by others and therefore allows him to clarify or to rectify them.

Very often, we may learn a lot about ourselves from negative feedback and it may help us sometimes to avoid wrongdoing.

Generally when we receive a gift, we thank the donor.

This is exactly what we should be doing when receiving constructive feedback from a friend, a relative or a colleague at work.

Why don't we do it ?

Basically because we believe so strongly in our own opinion, judgement, actions, that we have a difficulty to question them.

Accepting negative feedback and expressing thanks for it is not easy, particularly when we thought we had it right !

Feedback sometimes obliges us to change our "mind" and realise that we were not 100% right and may even be quite wrong.

Who likes to be proven wrong ? Not many people, if anyone.

That is the reason why negative feedback should be prepared carefully according to the personality of the reciepient, her culture, her degree of selfesteem and ability to take it in a positive way.

This is true for giving feedback downwards, but even more so when giving feedback upwards (to one's boss, parent, people we depend on).

And also when giving feedback to friends, colleagues, brother or sister.

If not done correctly, feedback might be rejected and generate frustration and a grudge and sometimes even lead to the breakdown of the relationship.

When Kenneth Blanchard wrote his famous book "The one minute manager", he called feedback "the breakfast of champions" because artists, sport athletes and managers should consider feedback as a gift to become a champion.

Do you want to become a champion in whatever you do ? Then request and take feedback positively from your peers, coach, friends.

Let us take it as a gift and get rid of defensiveness.

Instead of questioning it, let us thank for it !

CHAPTER 2

Positive and Negative Feedback

Feedback can be positive or negative and sometimes it is a combination of both, in a performance appraisal meeting for example.

Positive feedback is generally well received by most people because it is pleasant to hear and because it consolidates one's selfesteem.

But some people tend to be defensive when they get positive feedback either because they think that it is not deserved or because they suspect some kind of manipulation: "by congratulating me on this, what is she trying to provoke or what is she going to request from me later ?" are some reflections not always expressed but often felt.

People who tend to react negatively to positive feedback should not be deprived of such feedback because the reason of their attitude might be that they themselves have a difficulty to give genuine positive feedback and because they might themselves tend to use positive feedback to manipulate people.

In fact everyone needs both positive and negative (we prefer to call it constructive) feedback in order to progress.

Too much negative feedback might discourage the receiver and even demotivate him.

Too much positive feedback might lead the receiver to question the sincerity of the giver. Moreover it does not help change, so it is not very useful !

Therefore positive and negative feedback should be balanced if the purpose is to reinforce a relationship.

But this balancing is not easy because we are generally either positive or negative feedback-oriented.

People who are positive feedback-oriented are people who tend to see more the positive in life than the negative. They are often easygoing and "cool" and want to generate a good atmosphere. These people are liked, but because they do not give much negative feedback, they do not generate change in others.

People who are negative feedback oriented are generally very demanding from others and often as well as from themselves. They constantly challenge people reporting to them (colleagues, kids, friends) and are never 100% satisfied with their achievements.

For them, doing things well is just "normal" and it should not be a reason for getting positive feedback !

But because they are not there to give positive strokes when deserved, they miss good opportunities to raise the morale of their people.

Being able to give both negative and positive feedback when deserved is not easy: few people can do it because it requires a balanced personality as well as a capacity to evaluate the efforts put by others behind their actions.

Good parents and good managers should precisely be capable of measuring efforts not only results: they should look behind achievements, good or bad, and appreciate efforts even if these efforts have not lead to results yet.

These managers, parents, supervisors have understood that, if you want your negative feedback to be accepted, you also have to give positive feedback when deserved. Since, if people need to be challenged, they also need to be reassured by hearing nice words that tell them that their efforts have been noticed and appreciated.

An ability to give balanced feedback is what all managers should work on: It is the not easy but it is the best way to keep people motivated and willing to exceed expectations.

CHAPTER 3

Learning through Feedback

Learning by oneself through introspection (looking into oneself) is certainly a good thing to do.

Questioning one's opinions and comparing ourselves with great achievers and heroes to see what they would do in a similar situation is also good.

Before taking important decisions, it is well known that great leaders like JFK or Charles De Gaulle used to retire for a day or two in the countryside to think about possible alternatives before taking a stand on a controversial issue or taking and then announcing an important and final decision.

So thinking by oneself without discussing too long with others can be a good way to mature a decision. It is also a good way to avoid being overly influenced by others.

Some people call this process "listening to your inner voice" and we certainly should do it in some occasions.

But the danger of staying at the "self learning" stage is that, when things become really critical, it prevents us from investigating the pros and cons of alternatives that did not come to our own mind.

In such situations, feedback from someone else might help us identify some underestimated variables that, if not taken into account, could torpedo our plan.

Moreover, looking at a situation from different angles might help take into account other aspects of it, and therefore asking for feedback (in this case a critical view to the decision before it is even made), is very advisable when faced with a complex issue.

Now it is obviously important to also make sure that feedback is not biased and that the person whose feedback has been requested has no hidden agenda.

That is why, rather than sharing our thoughts always with the same person, it is advisable to discuss situations with different people in order to make sure that all angles of the situation have been considered.

To conclude, the best decisions are taken after they have been discussed with advisors with good judgement.

And then, After such a discussion, two situations can happen:

First, after soliciting different opinions, you have come to the conclusion that your initial plan should be amended:

In this case, amend it and move ahead.

But if, after carefully listening to everyone, you are not convinced by what you heard and your "gutsfeeling" tells you to pursue your initial idea, then move ahead and follow your intuition !

After all, advisors are not accountable for your actions.

And at the end of the day, You and nobody else will have to face the critics, negative judgements and possible counter actions due to your possible wrong decision or wrongdoing.

Now, getting away from big issues and back to our daily life, asking for regular feedback from others is advisable for two main reasons:

ONE, BECAUSE OUR BEHAVIOUR HAS AN IMPACT ON OTHERS...

and to live in harmony with others, it is important to know what impact we have on them and why.

In too many situations, our intentions were good but our actions were not perceived as such by people around us.

Conclusion: learning how we are perceived is essential to live in harmony.

TWO, BECAUSE ASKING FOR FEEDBACK WILL HELP CONVINCE OTHERS.

Since our objective is often to influence others, their perception of what we did, said, or revealed will ultimately impact their understanding and their reactions: asking for feedback is therefore necessary to understand and then to influence others.

Therefore FEEDBACK SHOULD NOT BE CONSIDERED AS A DUE. It should really be taken as a "gift" because when people (our boss, our peer, our life companion) accepts to give us honest feedback, they give us, free of charge, a unique opportunity to learn and change.

A simple example: if more than one of our peers tell us that our newly grown whiskers make us look older and dirty, should' nt we reward them by a big "THANKS" rather than arguing or rejecting their opinion ?

CHAPTER 4

Why is Feedback often Rejected

Positive feedback is generally well accepted because it is pleasant to hear positive statements about us, what we said or did, and there is normally no reason to suspect any negative intention except when positive feedback is given in a sarcastic tone. (But then it is not positive any more.)

On the contrary, in many circumstances, negative feedback is not well received, particularly when it was not solicited.

My neighbour is mowing his grass on Sunday morning and this is against the local law. I am very upset and take my phone to tell him to stop immediately, otherwise I shall call the police !

Obviously, my neighbour is not going to apologise and stop. On the contrary, there is a good chance that he ignores my feedback and threat and continues mowing his grass !

By calling and threatening him, I will probably just get the opposite of what I was expecting because I made 3 big mistakes: a) I called him by phone instead of going to his place (lack of respect) b) I did not start by any positive opening. Instead I started by aggressing him c) I did not try to find out why he was mowing his grass on Sunday morning: maybe there was a good reason for it ...maybe he had no other choice ....

In order to improve my feedback to him, I should have visited him, waited for him to stop the engine to be able to listen to me, then express my dissatisfaction about the noise, explain why the noise was particularly disagreeable on Sunday morning and ask him if it would be possible to wait until Monday to get his grass mowed.

In this example, we are talking about two people not reporting to one another.

But when feedback comes from a superior, as we mentioned before, more complex psychological factors interfere.

a) parent to child : the feeling of not beeing understood (generation conflict)

b) parent to child in law: the feeling of not beeing loved

c) manager to staff: the feeling of not beeing appreciated or recognised

d) officer to soldier: the feeling of rigidity, stubbornness

e) teacher to pupil : the feeling of dominance, dislike of non-parental authority

f) police officer to teenagers: the feeling of being discriminated etc...

Not to mention the rejection of feedback coming from authorities from another country/culture... (He takes it out on me because I am black, a jew, an immigrant, a woman, a roma etc..)

Here comes another factor for feedback to be accepted: it should be given by someone, I feel, has the right to give it to me.

And never in front of my friends, strangers, colleagues, brother or sister:

Feedback should be given through direct eye contact to avoid feeling of humiliation.

So all the reasons why feedback is not welcome have to be understood and respected.

In most cases the person who is giving feedback is just thinking of himself, his interest, the (perceived or real) damage done to him.

To sum up, giving feedback in the proper way is probably one of the most difficult communication exercise because so many factors and precautions should be taken into account to make it work as expected.

This is probably the reason why so many people do not like to give feedback.

Some people hate giving constructive feedback so much that they just do not give any feedback at all.

Let us be honest with ourselves:

We do not generally like lessons, advices and judgements coming from others.

Even good friends should be careful when giving their opinion when not asked to do so. In any case, make sure not to become judgemental because we all hate to be judged by others.

Yes, good friends should be capable of speaking freely to each other.

But if you want to keep a good friend, replace judgements by understanding and be more empathetic than critical.

CHAPTER 5

The 4 Ways to Improve Oneself

If we look at life and the occasions to learn, there are 4 main ways to improve oneself:

a) education through parents and educators

b) learning through experiences (with or without the intervention of others)

c) learning from books, films, seminars, conferences etc...

d) feedback from others in our professional and private life
(boss, peers, strangers, companion, friends etc...)

a) Education through parents and educators is essential because it takes place at a very early age and therefore has a long and strong lasting effect on personality.

In fact values, like respect for others, come from this period of life which starts as soon as we are one year old and maybe even earlier.

If those important values have not been transmitted at this ealier age, there are good chances that they will never be.

That is why families and kindergarden continue have an essential role in socializing people.

b) Learning through one's own experience is essential.

To my young little boy who shows an interest for the hot oven, nothing will be as effective to prevent him from touching it again than a first trial !

Experience is a good teacher in a lot of other circumstances., provided that we learn from them.

c) Learning from books, films, conferences and seminars is, of course, very important and even more now since internet provides access to tons of information, knowledge and knowhow !

This is so true today that anyone in the world can learn from his home about any subject.

Will this make people better ? Or worse ? It all depends on our own choices.

Are we interested to learn how to make a mini nuclear bomb or eighteen century French painting ? Both topics are on the internet !

Here again comes education and how to use internet in the best possible way.

d) Feedback from others

As mentioned earlier, for us, feedback from others is essential for two reasons:

- it is difficult to questions oneself without knowing how others perceive us.

- by beeing open to others' feedback we show the way and encourage others to sollicit our feedback in return. We therefore initiate a "feedback culture"

which will benefit our partnership or community (family, company, association, club etc..)

CHAPTER 6

Giving Feedback that Works

Whether you are a bishop, a manager or a parent, the people you deal with at some point deserve feedback from you, positive and negative.

And if you want to keep a good relationship with them, it is your duty to give feedback as often as needed.

As we mentioned before, in order to get your negative feedback accepted by your subordinate, do not hesitate to give positive feedback whenever it is deserved, for this will reduce resistance to negative feedback by helping subordinate keep a high level of self confidence.

And we know that lack of self-confidence is one of the reasons why people tend to reject feedback.

So how should we give feedback to make it work ?

Each one of the five following steps is important:

STEP 1 ASK FOR PERMISSION

It sounds strange, but it is a very good idea if you want to increase the chances that your feedback will be positively received.

By asking for permission, even if the question is rhethorical, we show respect to the person we want to give feedback to.

Who am I to give feedback to a person who does not want it ?

What right do I have to judge with my values, principles, education, culture ?

Asking for permission can be short and to the point like:

"Would you like to hear my view about the way you led your meeting yesterday" ?

STEP 2 EXPRESS WHAT YOU OBSERVED WITHOUT JUDGEMENT

Do not hesitate to express what you observed without "beating around the bush"and with as many details and concrete facts as possible.

However try to be as neutral and descriptive as possible and avoid judgement.

Example: instead of "I do not like your attitude these days", say:

"I was very surprised by your negative attitude during the conclusion of our meeting yesterday"

And then listen to what your child, staff member, employee has to say....

STEP 3 PINPOINT THE IMPACT

In most cases, people do not do or say negative things just for the sake of it !

The impact of what they did was very often minimized or even not seen at all.

That is why the necessary time should be used to pinpoint the impact of a negative act on other people, the organisation, the family etc..

Example: "By not observing the deadline that you had committed to, do you realise that you are upsetting all your colleagues' work ?"

STEP 4 LET PEOPLE REACT

Allowing people to react and listening carefully to their reaction, without interrupting them is the best way to show respect to the other party and to make sure that you understand the reason of the mistake/error.

It is not easy, but any guilty person has the right to speak and defend herself in any jurisdiction. Why should it be different in our organisation or family ?

There is only one exception to this rule: if the defendant shows ill faith and starts putting all the blame on others without accepting any responsibility for what happens:

In such a case, we have the right to interrupt in order for us to express our view and stop ill-faithy arguments.

STEP 5 ASK FOR PROPOSAL(S)

Once you have expressed your feelings and opinion and listened to the other person's point of view, the time has come to look for solutions on how to put the negative behind and prepare for the future.

"What do you suggest" is often the best question to ask in order to get the solution from the person who is responsible for what happened.

It makes your subordinate, child, friend, accountable for finding and implementing a solution and gives him a chance to solve the problem by himself, which is a good way of respecting his territory and helping him safeguard his self-confidence.

Obviously, you may suggest the next steps if needed, but not before inviting your subordinate to come up with a solution first.

These five steps are magical. They work in practically all cases if they are properly followed.

CHAPTER 7

The Particularity of Giving Feedback Downwards

What we call downwards feedback is a feedback given by someone in a higher position (parents, boss, employer, army officer etc...).

The particularity of this type of feedback is that it is hard to reject verbally because of the relation of dependence between the person who delivers feedback and the one who receives it.

If I reject the feedback given by my boss, what will happen to me ?

Is she going to sanction me at the next occasion ? Will it hurt our relationship for good ? Is she going to put an end to our relation ?

Because of this unequal relationship, it is risky to contest the content of the feedback received. So the temptation is to accept it verbally, but not genuinely and do nothing to change. Or, even worse, to challenge the facts as they are described and adopt a defensive or even fighting posture.

So the degree of acceptating of downwards feedback depends very much on the way it has been expressed by the giver, but also on the personality of the receiver and the culture of the organisation where both giver and receiver interact.

In a high-tech company with open communication and low hierarchy, negative feedback will, in most cases, be accepted as a normal process.

In a more conservative environment, with high hierarchy levels, feedback from a boss is like coming from god himself: it should not be discussed or argued.

In the army, the situation is similar as it is within families with very authoritative parents with a conservative culture.

In such human communities, feedback should not be challenged. It should just be accepted even if unfair and not deserved.

Personality also plays an important role in taking feedback positively or not:

People with high self-confidence and who are eager to learn tend to accept and use feedback to grow.

People less sure of themselves tend to resist negative feedback because it puts into question and may downgrade their self-image.

Therefore, before giving feedback, as we mentioned before, it is preferable to ask for permission through a question like "would you be interested to hear what I think of the way you have managed this situation" ?

If the question is answered by "yes", it will be more difficult for the recipient to reject the content of the message.

If it is answered by "no", a "why" question becomes necessary in order to find out why feedback is not welcome at this moment.

Now obviously a boss, parent, officer does not have to ask for permission, before giving feedback. But it is up to them to give feedback in such a way, with the right balance between positive and negative words, that it becomes a real gift, a precious benefit for the receiver, a "champions' breakfast" !

CHAPTER 8

Feedback and Teamwork

Within a team, the way members give and accept feedback from each other is very revealing. It is a good indicator of the level of team spirit.

Within a team, feedback is important for two main reasons:

A) IT ALLOWS TEAM MEMBERS WHO ARE OPEN TO IT TO USE IT AS A GREAT LEARNING TOOL.

To understand the power of feedback, just think of what often happens to people who are not open to it !

Some bosses love to be surrounded by "yes people" e.g people who always support them whatever they say or do and never bring them any contradiction.

A "yes man organisation" can live for some time if the leader is a visionary.

But one day, even a great visionary can be wrong... and then, what will happen if no-one dares to come up and contradict the leader's view before it is too late ?

The whole company might go wrong and the risks of making bad decisions and running into the wall is huge.

Example: the Shah of Iran was surrounded by "yes people". He wanted his followers to adhere to his thoughts and decisions to the point that nobody would dare to tell him that there was a silent conspiring from the Islamic clergy exploiting the discontent of the population.

The day the Shah realised what was happening, it was already too late.

If the Shah of Iran would have been able to listen to negative feedback from some of his officers, he would probably have learnt from it and his son might be ruling the country today !

B) REQUESTING AND ACCEPTING FEEDBACK AND USING IT IS PROBABLY THE BEST WAY TO CONSOLIDATE GOOD RELATIONSHIP WITHIN THE TEAM.

We are not alone on this planet. The success of our life depends very much on our ability to build positive, long lasting relationships with others.

How can this be achieved without welcoming feedback from friends, companions, family, boss, colleagues and taking it positively ?

This does not mean that the one who spoke last should be right and that we should change our opinion after listening to Peter, Paul or Jack.

But what happens to people who react defensively to feedback ?

Just think of a team where some members take feedback well and use it to improve whereas others are resisting feedback and systematically defend themselves: after some times the leader of this team will continue to give feedback to the team members who take it positively and stop feedback to others. (it is so discouraging to face defensiveness from people we want to help !)

What will happen after a while is that part of the team will get better and better while the rest will stop growing.

And what about relationships within such a team ? Can we still speak of team spirit ? And what about the performances of the two parts of the team ?

Therefore the ability to take and give feedback to one another is an essential condition for team success. There is no better way to improve relationship AND performance within a team.

To conclude, it should be one of the priorities of a team leader to build within his team a "feedback culture" by which feedback is constantly requested and positively accepted by all.

And the example should come from the top: If it does, the whole company becomes a "learning organisation" where everyone learns from the experience of each other.

CHAPTER 9

The Courage to ask for and Accept Feedback

Positive and negative feedback should not only be given downwards.

The process can and should go the other way !

But obviously this is trickier especially when the person you want to give feedback to has a big ego and does not appreciate to be challenged.

And this can be due to a number of reasons such as:

-That person is convinced that he knows it all !

-The culture of the organisation is very hierarchical and bosses are considered as infallible.

-The person is not open to criticism.

-The person has a difficulty to question herself.

-She looks like a strong boss, but in fact, she is not so sure of herself and is afraid of losing face...

But the problem can also come from the one who delivers feedback:

She may lack courage and prefers to keep quite.

She could be affraid of offending her boss, parent, superior.

She does not want to contradict her superior in front of colleagues.

Or she simply never learnt how to give feedback....

To conclude, it is a fact that giving negative feedback upwards can be risky and is difficult to perform well.

And you need COURAGE to ask and to give feedback in many situations and particularly upwards.

It is so much easier to shut up and keep your opinion for yourself when you feel that challenging is not welcome !

Unfortunately this attitude of keeping quite rather than opening up and criticizing positively is very frequent in a number of cultures because people who take the risk of expressing feedback upwards are not appreciated for it and even sometimes loses out on promotion to more docile employees.

They realise that although feedback is officially advocated, in reality, only positive comments are welcome.

In such organisations, people tend to adopt a "yes man" attitude and their leader, deprived from salutary contradiction, has no way to check the rightness of his opinions/decisions.

Openness and speaking freely are the attributes of peak performing companies.

In those organisations, self-censorship does not exist.

" If a boss and his deputy never disagree on anything, the proverb says, one of the two is too many ! "

Sorry to say, but in this case, the boss is useless for he never uses his staff members' brain to question his decisions.

By not accepting constructive feedback from his deputies, there are good chances that he misses out on some interesting idea that could have made his organisation much more successful !

CHAPTER 10

Following up on Feedback

Requesting, giving and receiving feedback is not always easy, but it can be an essential factor of success within a team, a family, a company.

However all depends on whether or not feedback is being followed up and how it is used by the receivers.

Often, we pretend to take it positively in order to keep the peace, but, deep down, we cannot avoid to challenge its validity and keep on doing things as before.

For receivers, feedback will only be useful if it generates questions and leads to a change of behaviour. Otherwise it is useless !

For leaders whose job is to give relevant feedback to their staff members, communicating feedback is not enough.

The leader's job is to check that feedback is taken seriously into account by the receiver and that it really generates substantial behavioural changes.

When it does, it is important to notice the change and acknowledge it by some supportive statement like: "I saw that you took into account what we discussed yesterday and made efforts to change, this way makes you look much better and you should pursue what you started !"

To change habits is sometimes very difficult and people who are capable of identifying bad habits thanks to others' feedback and to correct them deserve positive appreciation.

In sports, for example, one of the main roles of a coach is to help trainees become conscious of what they can do to become more efficient and the best coaches are the ones who can just do that.

As a parent, manager, professor things are very much the same.

And the teachers that we remember the most are the ones who were tough with us and insisted to see us change.

"Management, Peter Drucker use to say, is nothing else than identifying what someone is capable of doing and when we have identified it, insist that they DO IT ! "

So implementing change is what counts, not just being aware of what we could change. And this is true not only for individuals, but also for organisations. That is why feedback and follow up on feedback are the two basic success factors in today's business world.

As a parent, a boss, a coach, make sure that your trainee remembers you for ever because of the role you have been playing as a change catalyst through demanding leadership based on continuous feedback.

www.ingramcontent.com/pod-product-compliance
Lightning Source LLC
Chambersburg PA
CBHW070726180526
45167CB00004B/1630